In Good Company

Some Personal Recollections of Swinburne, Lord Roberts, Watts-Dunton, Oscar Wilde, Edward Whymper, S. J. Stone, Stephen Phillips

Coulson Kernahan

Contents

Bibliographic Key Phrases   1

Publisher's Note   3

Historical Context   5
    A Work of Its Time 5
    A Window Into the Past 6
    A Work for the Present 6
    A Work for the Future 8

Abstracts   11
    TLDR (three words) 11
    ELI5 11
    Scientific-Style Abstract 12
    For Complete Idiots Only 12

Learning Aids	**13**
Mnemonic (acronym)	13
Mnemonic (speakable)	13
Mnemonic (singable)	14
Most Important Passages	**17**
Swinburne's Power of Concentration and Memory:	17
Watts-Dunton's "Good Fellowship" Creed:	19
The True Test of Success:	19
Lord Roberts's Unfailing Consideration: . .	20
The Value of Unspoken Words:	21
Watts-Dunton's Unwavering Loyalty: . . .	23
The Power of Poetry:	24
Condensed Matter	**27**
A.C. Swinburne	27
Lord Roberts	30
Theodore Watts-Dunton as the "Ogre of the 'Athenæum'"	33
Why Theodore Watts-Dunton Published Only Two Books	36
Theodore Watts-Dunton as an Amateur in Authorship and as a Good Fellow . . .	38
One Aspect of the Many-Sidedness of Theodore Watts-Dunton	40
The Last Days of Theodore Watts-Dunton .	41
When Stephen Phillips Read	45
Edward Whymper as I Knew Him	46

Oscar Wilde	52
S.J. Stone, the Hymn-Writer	54
Browsable Glossary	**57**
Timeline	**83**

Bibliographic Key Phrases

Literary friendship; English poet; Religious drama; Irish humor; Victorian England; National Service; Anglo-Saxon Celt; Great Mountaineer; Literary Ogre; Bohemian life; Lost poems; Book of Job; Good-fellowship of God; First Principles; Literary shop; Soul of man; Child at play;

Publisher's Note

Imagine if Oscar Wilde had been your friend! In a world increasingly consumed by digital distractions and fleeting trends, it's easy to forget the enduring power of meaningful connection. This book, *In Good Company*, offers a poignant antidote, taking us on a journey into the heart of a bygone era where friendship and personal connection reigned supreme. Coulson Kernahan, a master storyteller himself, paints intimate portraits of his remarkable contemporaries, each a luminary in their field–poets, soldiers, critics, and adventurers–revealing the complexities and brilliance that resided beyond their public personas.

Through insightful anecdotes and compelling letters, Kernahan brings these figures to life, capturing the essence of their personalities, their wit, their vulnerabilities, and their profound impact on the world. He delves into the heart of their friendships, highlighting the enduring power of loyalty, respect, and the shared pursuit of intellectual and artistic excellence, offering a glimpse into the rich tapestry of human connection that has shaped our cultural landscape.

This book is a must-read for anyone seeking a deeper understanding of the human condition, the nuances of friendship, and the enduring power of the written word. Readers will gain a unique perspective on the lives and works of these extraordinary individuals, learn about their creative processes and their relationships, and perhaps even be inspired to foster more meaningful connections in their own lives.

Historical Context

A Work of Its Time

Coulson Kernahan's *In Good Company* (1917) is a collection of essays about the personalities of eight men who were prominent in the cultural life of late Victorian England: Algernon Charles Swinburne, Lord Roberts, Theodore Watts-Dunton, Oscar Wilde, Edward Whymper, and S. J. Stone, as well as Stephen Phillips. The work is a kind of *Who's Who* of Victorian and Edwardian literary and social life, and Kernahan's portraits of his friends are filled with anecdotes about their individual habits and personalities. It is notable that Kernahan was a younger man during this period, and that his work in this book is generally considered a kind of "apprenticeship" for the longer, more detailed *Recollections* he is planning, which will no doubt be the more significant literary work.

A Window Into the Past

In Good Company was a success in its time, not only for the well-known names Kernahan discusses, but for the glimpses into the lives of people who were important in the cultural world of that era but who have since fallen into obscurity. The book also illustrates several features of the literary world of the late Victorian era: the intense friendships and the fierce rivalries; the emphasis on good fellowship and the gentlemanly conduct expected of literary men; and the cult of celebrity, which was even more intense in this era than it has become in our own times. The social and literary world of this time was a world that has disappeared; and *In Good Company* is an indispensable window into that lost world, and one that is still illuminating for understanding the Victorian cultural scene, and the Edwardian era that followed it.

A Work for the Present

In Good Company might seem to be a book of interest only to literary historians; but as the book is full of personal vignettes, anecdotes, and even gossip that will interest those who have not made a particular study of Victorian literature, it is also a book that will be appreciated by general readers.

The Cult of Celebrity

It is interesting to note that *In Good Company* was written just after the First World War, an era that in some ways saw the end of the cult of the celebrity and its replacement by more "serious" cultural and social concerns. Kernahan describes a world in which men and women were more preoccupied with the social and literary "in" crowd than they are today. This may be of interest to those who would understand our own present obsession with celebrities in the entertainment world, and the emphasis placed upon the personal life of celebrities.

The Importance of Biography

In Good Company is in part a collection of biographical sketches, but it is also a significant early exploration of the relationship between personality and art. It is particularly interesting for its exploration of how personality affects the art, or the craft of the writer, poet, and artist. The influence of one man's personality on another, which is illustrated in the book, may be of interest to those who seek to understand how individuals who are "influential" shape or distort the work of others.

The Problem of Morality

In a world seemingly obsessed by the idea of morality and of the nature of human sin, Kernahan's *In Good Company* is a book that may provide some insight into the moral nature of the men about whom he writes. He writes of men who might be considered "immoral" but whose lives and characters are not seen through a single lens of judgment. Kernahan provides a glimpse into the lives of men whose moral shortcomings are not hidden or romanticized but are viewed with a complex mixture of judgment, sympathy, and a sense of the tragic.

A Work for the Future

In future decades, *In Good Company* may be of interest to readers who are seeking to understand the social, cultural, and political forces that shaped Victorian England and the period that followed it. Kernahan provides unique insights into the literary world of the late Victorian era, but it is also a book that will resonate with those who are interested in the dynamics of the individual, of fame, and of the nature of human relationships. As the world continues to move at ever-increasing speed, the past may provide valuable insights into the present, and the future may find that the world of the late Victorian era is no less complex and no less relevant than it was over a century ago.

Abstracts

TLDR (three words)

Literary friendships remembered

ELI5

This is a book about the author's friends. He writes about famous people like poets, soldiers, and artists. He tells stories about them and how they were in real life.

Scientific-Style Abstract

This book, *In Good Company*, is a collection of biographical sketches of notable figures from the late Victorian and Edwardian eras. The author, Coulson Kernahan, reflects on his personal relationships with these individuals and offers intimate glimpses into their personalities. Through anecdotes, letters, and observations, Kernahan reveals the complexities and nuances of these figures, often challenging conventional perceptions. He highlights the intellectual vibrancy, eccentricities, and profound humanity of his subjects, revealing them as individuals rather than mere historical figures. The collection provides a unique and engaging perspective on a significant period in British literary and cultural history.

For Complete Idiots Only

The author is explaining the differences between the personalities of people considered "geniuses" (super smart, creative people) and "normal" people. He is saying that geniuses are not as well-behaved as normal people, and can get angry, upset, or act irrationally more easily than normal people.

Learning Aids

Mnemonic (acronym)

SWOWLERP - Swinburne, Watts-Dunton, Oscar Wilde, Lord Roberts, Edward Whymper, Stephen Phillips, S. J. Stone.

Mnemonic (speakable)

A Swirling Sea of Greatness - Swinburne, Watts-Dunton, Oscar Wilde, Lord Roberts, Edward Whymper, Stephen Phillips, S. J. Stone.

Mnemonic (singable)

(To the tune of "The Wheels on the Bus")

Swinburne was a poet, a poet, a poet

Swinburne was a poet, full of fire

Watts-Dunton was his friend, his friend, his friend

Watts-Dunton was his friend, a great soul

Oscar Wilde was a wit, a wit, a wit

Oscar Wilde was a wit, a charming fellow

Lord Roberts was a soldier, a soldier, a soldier

Lord Roberts was a soldier, true to duty

Edward Whymper was a climber, a climber, a climber

Edward Whymper was a climber, a brave soul

Stephen Phillips was a reader, a reader, a reader

Stephen Phillips was a reader, magical voice

S. J. Stone was a parson, a parson, a parson

S. J. Stone was a parson, with a kind heart

In good company, in good company

In good company, they lived and died

In good company, in good company

In good company, their lives we prize.

Most Important Passages

Swinburne's Power of Concentration and Memory:

Swinburne's remarks upon the subject of my article–though I need hardly say I have forgotten no word of what he said–I pass over, but what I must not pass over is the witness these remarks bore to his extraordinary memory and to his equally extraordinary method of reading. Reading, in fact, is not the word. Had he parsed the article, schoolboy wise, sentence by sentence, he could not more effectually have mastered it; had he dissected it, part by part, surgeon-like, he could not more completely have torn the heart out of the matter.

Obviously Swinburne could only have read the thing once, yet had I, the writer, been called upon, even while it was fresh in my memory, to pass an examination on this very article, I doubt whether I should have known half as much of it as he. Hearing him thus deliver himself upon a casual contribution to a periodical, which, by reason of his love and friendship for the blind poet with whom the article dealt, had chanced to interest him, I could understand how his single brain had been able to deal illuminatingly with so vast a volume of literature as he had from time to time passed under review. His power of concentration, and of pouncing, hawk-like, upon what seemed to him to be memorable or salient, as well as his ability to recollect all he had read, must have been extraordinary. (Chapter 1, Section 4)

This passage emphasizes Swinburne's unusual memory and reading process. Kernahan is astounded that Swinburne can recall the contents of an article he has only read once, and then analyze it so completely. This ability, Kernahan argues, explains how Swinburne could have been so prolific and insightful as a critic.

Watts-Dunton's "Good Fellowship" Creed:

> "My theory always is that a winsome style in prose comes from a man whose heart is good." I had shown appreciation of his friend, and, partisan and hero of friendship that he was, he was willing to take the rest on trust. Rightly to appreciate his friend was to win Watts-Dunton's heart at the start. (Chapter 6, Section 1)

This passage encapsulates Watts-Dunton's central belief—that good-fellowship is more important than genius. His kindness to Kernahan because he showed appreciation for Robinson, a mutual friend, demonstrates how this principle guided his behavior.

The True Test of Success:

> But a success deservedly won, even if a so-called popular success, every writer in his heart desires. To pretend otherwise

> is mere insincerity. It is not "playing the game," for even the pursuit of Letters is none the worse for a touch of the English sporting spirit. It is indeed the chief reproach of those of us who follow the craft of Letters that we are "artists" rather than sportsmen. Englishmen fight the better and write the better for seeing alike in writing and in fighting something of a "game." (Chapter 6, Section 1)

Kernahan argues that all writers desire success, whether popular or critical, and to deny this is insincere. He compares the competitive spirit of writing to that of sport, arguing that writers are better for embracing the competition.

Lord Roberts's Unfailing Consideration:

> Other men as greatly concerned in great matters as Lord Roberts was cannot always spare time to acknowledge and to show appreciation of work for a good cause, which is brought directly to their notice. Lord Roberts could find time, or perhaps I should say made time to write graciously about work the doer or the

> author of which had done nothing to bring that work under the Field-Marshal's eye. (Chapter 2, Section 1)

This passage illustrates Lord Roberts's character. Despite being a very busy man, he took time to acknowledge and commend a writer for work he had not been asked to review.

The Value of Unspoken Words:

> So, of Wilde himself, I cannot but hope and believe that though he told many stories of exceeding beauty, none of which were true, yet hidden away in his heart was much that was gracious, true, noble and beautiful, the story of which will now never be known, for like the poet lad of his fantasy he told it to no one. Of what was evil and what was good in his life, only a merciful God can strike the balance, and only a merciful God shall judge. (Chapter 8, Section 5)

Kernahan's conclusion about Wilde is that even a man who has committed great crimes is capable of goodness and beauty that never comes to light. He acknowledges that only God can judge Wilde's life. This passage is important because it demonstrates Kernahan's compassionate, merciful perspective.

Here are two more passages about Oscar Wilde:

Wilde's Paradoxical Nature:

> "Was it not Mr. Stead who defined paradox as a truth standing on its head? Wilde's aim in paradox was so to manipulate truth and falsehood as to make the result startle one by appearing to reverse the existing standard. A paradox by him was sometimes a lie and a truth trotting side by side together in double harness like a pair of horses, but each so cleverly disguised that one was not quite sure which horse was which." (Chapter 8, Section 5)

This passage examines Wilde's tendency toward paradox, suggesting a deliberate blurring of truth and falsehood for artistic effect. It highlights his playful manipulation of language and his ability to challenge conventional perceptions.

Wilde's Complex Morality:

> "To the folk who objected that Wilde has boasted of being a "pagan" I replied that he probably used the word–just then very much in vogue–in the same sense in which

> Mr. Kenneth Grahame used it when he entitled a volume, bubbling over with the joy of life, with animal spirits, keen observation, and exquisite humour, *Pagan Papers*. Wilde's "paganism" I took as meaning no more than that he claimed for himself freedom from formula, most of all freedom from cant in his attitude towards the accepted conventions, whether literary, artistic, social, or even religious." (Chapter 8, Section 6)

Kernahan explores the complexities of Wilde's morality, suggesting that Wilde's "paganism" was more a rejection of dogma and hypocrisy than a true embrace of immorality. This passage attempts to provide a more nuanced perspective on Wilde's often-controversial views.

Watts-Dunton's Unwavering Loyalty:

> It was, indeed, always in defence of his friends, rarely if ever in defence of himself–though he was abnormally sensitive to adverse criticism–that he entered into a quarrel and, since dead friends could not defend themselves, he constituted himself

> the champion of their memory or of their reputation, and even steeled himself on more than one occasion to a break with a living friend rather than endure a slight to one who was gone. (Chapter 7, Section 1)

Kernahan describes Watts-Dunton's extraordinary loyalty. Watts-Dunton was willing to sacrifice his own relationships and even his own reputation to defend his friends. This passage is important because it highlights Watts-Dunton's commitment to his friendships.

The Power of Poetry:

> Poetry kindled the taper of his soul to flame, as only poetry could. His genius was more supremely evident at such times–that is to say, when he was *living* poetry, when he was, as it were, caught up and filled by some Pentecostal spirit of poetry outside himself–than when he was, in travail and labour, if under the pure impulse of inspiration, creating poetry. Then from the man to whom we were listening the fetters of the senses (alas, that those fetters should sometimes hold so closely and so heavily as to drag us downwards to earth!) seemed to fall away, and his soul to soar

back to the heaven whence he had fallen.
(Chapter 9, Section 2)

This passage describes the transcendent power of poetry to elevate Stephen Phillips. When reading, he is able to transcend the physical and experience a spiritual transformation. Kernahan compares his reading to a "Pentecostal spirit of poetry" taking hold of him, and concludes that Phillips was at his best when he was "living" poetry.

Condensed Matter

A.C. Swinburne

When a poet turns the searchlight of criticism upon himself, one must be interested. Swinburne, on occasion, was prone to angry outbursts. One day, he was furious at a poet who he felt had vulgarised his work.

"Of all my imitators, this fellow...is the most intolerable. I claim—and you, I know, will admit the justice of the claim—that perhaps the most distinctive characteristic of my work in poetry is that I have taken old and hackneyed metres, and have tried to transform them from a mere jingle, and a mere jig-jig, into music. This pestilent ape has vulgarised what I have done by servile imitations of my manner and of my methods; but, what I had transformed into music, he has transformed back into the vilest and most jigging of jingles."

Swinburne was also a great admirer of Christina Rossetti, whom he felt was a true poet. At a luncheon, he suddenly interrupted the conversation to read a poem of hers, "The Death of a Firstborn." "I won't read the third and last verse," he said, "One glance at it is sufficient to show that it is unequal, and that the poem would be stronger and finer by its omission. But for the happy folk who are able to think as she thinks, who believe as she believes on religious matters, the poem is of its kind perfect."

The man who lived in a world of books, was the most courteous of hosts. "To no one would he defer quite so graciously and readily, to no one was he so scrupulously courtly in his bearing, as to those who constituted the household in which he lived." Swinburne delighted in long walks, and would talk of little else. "There is no time like the morning for a walk!" he declared, turning to me with enthusiasm. "The sparkle, the exhilaration of it! I walk every morning of my life, no matter what the weather, pelting along all the time as fast as I can go; and it is entirely to my daily walk that I attribute my perfect health."

He also possessed a prodigious memory. One day, while discussing an article I had written on Philip Bourke Marston, Swinburne, who had known the blind poet since he was fourteen, delivered an exhaustive analysis of it. "When Gabriel spoke of Philip's poem, *The Rose and the Wind*, as 'worthy of Shakespeare in his subtlest lyrical mood,' he let his personal affection run away with his critical judgment."

While Swinburne was clearly a great force of intellect and imagination, he was also a man of great emotion.

"You, who know Walter's magnificent, magician-like power of concentrating into the fourteen lines of a sonnet what no other poet could have said with equal power and felicity in forty, will agree with me when I tell you what perhaps you do not know, for he never speaks of it himself. When he was a young man, he lost a manuscript book of poems of which he had no copy. By these lost poems the world is, I believe, as poor as if Gabriel Rossetti's early poems had never been recovered from his wife's coffin."

The child in him remained to the very end. "I write poetry, I suppose, to escape from boredom." And, "Warm as was my regard for Algernon Charles Swinburne the man, profound as is my admiration of him as a poet, I am not sure that to this child-side of him must not be attributed much that was noblest and most lovable in his noble and lovable personality, as well as much that was loftiest and most enduring in his work."

His love of poetry was as boundless as his love of children. "It is apparently too often a congenial task," says

George Eliot in her *Essay on Heine*, "to write severe words about the transgressions of men of genius; especially when the censor has the advantage of being himself a man of no genius, so that those transgressions seem to him quite gratuitous; he, forsooth, never lacerated anyone by his wit or gave irresistible piquancy to a coarse allusion; and his indignation is not mitigated by any knowledge of the temptation that lies in transcendent power."

"Great hearts go generally with great brains."

Lord Roberts

Lord Roberts was a man of extraordinary kindness. The field marshal, upon meeting a young artillery officer who felt it his duty to offer unsolicited advice, listened with quiet courtesy and amusement. "Of course I was, as you say, amused at the young man's assurance and confidence in his own military knowledge. Many very young men are prone either to too great diffidence or to too great assurance. I think, on the whole, I incline to envy the young man with plenty of assurance, especially as I was disposed to be diffident myself at his age, as many of us Irishmen, for all our seeming confidence, are. But in any case I owed it to you, who had introduced him, as well as to myself, to treat him outwardly at least with courtesy and consideration."

Lord Roberts was also a man of great action. One day, while celebrating his eightieth birthday, Lord Roberts stopped to help a young officer whose reserves were far away and unable to answer his signals. "You did the right and only thing in stopping my car," Lord Roberts wrote to the officer. "If ever you are this way and disengaged, I hope you will call and give me the pleasure of making the further acquaintance of so good and resourceful a soldier."

On another occasion, he wrote to the author, who had written an article on National Defence in the *London Quarterly Review*.

"I am *delighted* with the article itself, and with the very clear and convincing way in which you have put forward the advantages of military training and discipline for all our able-bodied young men as affecting not only the position of Great Britain as a World Power, but the individual moral and physical improvement of the men of the nation."

Lord Roberts followed the work of those who supported National Defence with great interest. He would often send telegrams and messages of encouragement to those who were speaking on the issue. "It is possible that in the bewildering happenings of the war and in the breathless interest with which, at its end, the shifting of frontiers and the striking of great balances will be watched, there is the danger, if only from reaction, that we slackly fall back into our previous national inertia and national apathy."

Lord Roberts was often accused of being a cynical man, but he always insisted that his words were based on his belief in England's need for preparation.

"Lord Roberts," I wrote, "claimed no such 'right' for any nation wantonly and wickedly to force war upon another. He pointed out that when one nation has decided, for reasons of her own (possibly because she is ambitious and determined to play a great part in history), to force a war upon another nation, which possibly may decide to resist, if only because she is determined to hold to her own–the policy is that adopted by Germany. That policy–as a student of history as well as a soldier, Lord Roberts had to admit that it is often a winning policy–is to strike at what has been called the selected moment, or in other words, when she (Germany) is at her strongest, and the nation which she wishes to overthrow is weak."

Lord Roberts, deeply religious, never wrote prayers for publication. "It is not, as you know, that I do not believe in prayer. I have humbly asked God's help and guidance in everything that I undertook all through my life, and never more so than now, when I am an old man, and His call may be very near. But—-" he hesitated a moment, "offering up a brief prayer–it may only be the words 'God help me!'–before going into action, or in some time of difficulty, is one thing; and sitting down to write, to print and publish a prayer for others is quite another thing–for a soldier, at least."

He was a man of great energy who followed a strict daily schedule. "If it will be saving you a railway journey–and I know what a busy man you are," he wrote, "to see me here at the Hotel, instead of at Ascot, by all means let it be so. But I am afraid, if not too early for you, it must be at 8.30 in the morning, as the rest of my day is already mapped out."

"Keep shield to breast, keep bright your sword, and drawn!" Rang out his answer. *"On the horizon's rim I see great armies gather, and the dim, Grey mists of Armageddon's bloody dawn!"*

Theodore Watts-Dunton as the "Ogre of the 'Athenæum'"

The author of *Aylwin* was, in his day, a man of mystery. He had made his home with Rossetti and Swinburne, and was a known acquaintance of Tennyson. In the last decade of the 19th century, many people believed that Watts-Dunton was avoiding publicity, and that he would publish no books. "It was not until the publication of *Aylwin* that the name of Theodore Watts, or as he afterwards elected to be called Watts-Dunton, became widely known outside what are sometimes not very felicitously described as "literary circles."

He had also been known to live with gypsies.

"He was known to be the personal friend of Tennyson, Matthew Arnold, James Russell Lowell, Browning, and William Morris. Dante Gabriel Rossetti and George Meredith had in the past made their home with him at Chelsea, and Swinburne had been his house mate for many years at Putney. Rossetti and Swinburne had written and spoken of him in terms which to outsiders seem extravagant, and both had dedicated some of their best work to him. It was also known that he had lived for some time with gipsies, was one of the three greatest living authorities on gipsy lore and the gipsy language, and had been the friend of George Borrow."

But Watts-Dunton also had a reputation as a literary "ogre," a name that haunted him throughout his life. "Everyone knows he is so insanely jealous of us younger men that he watches the publishers' lists for every book by a young poet of ability to pounce upon it, and to cut it up. What has he done, I should like to know, to give him the right to pronounce death sentences? Why, the fellow's never even published a book of his own."

This reputation was largely unfounded. In reality, Watts-Dunton was a champion of the younger generation.

"My sympathies, as you know, are all with the younger men. I love to see a young poet, or for the matter of that *any* young writer, get recognition."

His style of reviewing was unique. It was known for being insightful, learned, and comprehensive.

"I believe, indeed I am sure, that my methods of using a book as an illustration of some first principle in criticism gives it more importance, attracts to it more attention than any more businesslike review article of the ordinary kind would, because my speciality is known to be that of dealing with first principles."

"What the devil would these men have? I suppose we are all to fall at their feet as soon as they have written a few good verses and discuss them as we discuss Sophocles, Æschylus, and Sappho. Does this not corroborate what Swinburne was saying to you the other day about the modesty of the first-rate poet and the something else of the others?"

Why Theodore Watts-Dunton Published Only Two Books

Watts-Dunton, unlike many authors, did not readily publish his work. He was a master of procrastination, and would often rewrite and revise his work until the very last minute.

"Part definitely with a book, that it might go to press, he would not, so long as a chance remained of holding on to it, to dovetail in a poem or a prose passage, perhaps from something penned many years ago, or to rewrite, amend, or omit whole chapters. I have seen proofs of his as bewildering in the matter of what printers call "pulling copy about" as a jigsaw puzzle."

He would often discuss projects with friends, but then fail to follow through.

"The fact is that Watts-Dunton was gratified by the request and did not disguise his pleasure, for with all his vast learning and acute intellect there was a singular and childlike simplicity about him that was very lovable. Actually accept a commission to write the book in question he would not, but he was not unwilling to hear the proposed terms, and in fact seemed so attracted by, and so interested in, the project that the pleased publisher would leave, conscious of having done a good morning's work, and of having been the first to propose, and so practically to bespeak, a book that was already almost as good as written, already almost as good as published, already almost as good as an assured success."

His literary ambitions came too late in life.

"The extraordinary success of *Aylwin*, published, be it remembered–though some of us had been privileged to see it long before–in 1898, when the author was 66, bewildered and staggered Watts-Dunton, but the literary ambitions which that success aroused came too late in life to be realised."

Watts-Dunton was a man of great friendships. "His best books stand upon our shelves in every part of the English-speaking world, but the name that appears upon the cover is not that of Theodore Watts-Dunton, but of Dante Gabriel Rossetti and Algernon Charles Swinburne. He wrote no Life of either, but how much of their life and of their life's best work we owe to Watts-Dunton we shall never know."

"His life-work, I repeat, was not literature nor poetry, but friendship."

He was also a man of great kindness, and would often go out of his way to help struggling writers and artists. "What he once said of Tennyson is equally true of Watts-Dunton himself. "When I first knew Tennyson," he said, "I was, if possible, a more obscure literary man than

I now am, and he treated me with exactly the same manly respect that he treated the most illustrious people."

"To my sorrow," he writes in a letter, "I was driven to quarrel with a man I loved and who loved me, William Minto, because he, with no ill intentions, printed certain injurious comments upon Rossetti which he found in Bell Scott's papers."

Theodore Watts-Dunton as an Amateur in Authorship and as a Good Fellow

Watts-Dunton was a man of great fellowship. His love of good-fellowship often led him to champion those who were struggling to make their way in the world.

"The one thing of all others upon which Watts-Dunton set store was good-fellowship, which he counted as of greater worth even than genius. If ever he went critically astray, if ever intellectually he overrated his man, it was because he allowed his heart to outride his head."

In his early days, he had befriended F.W. Robinson, who was then working on a magazine called *Home Chimes*. "The first letter he ever wrote to me (in sending me his novel *No Church*) I answered at the end of six months. I wish I could help it, but I can't. My friends have to take me with all my infirmities on my head."

Watts-Dunton was a man of great honesty, and he did not pretend to be indifferent to the success he achieved.

"He was transparently ingenuous of thought and purpose and did not attempt to conceal his gratification at the success of *Aylwin* or the pleasure which a discriminating and sympathetic appreciation afforded him."

"Your shrewd professional writer would have spent less time in contemplation of his success, and more in seeking how best to exploit and advertise that success to his professional advantage."

"Watts-Dunton, on the contrary, took the success of *Aylwin* very much as a young mother takes her firstling. He dandled it, toyed with it, hugged it, not altogether without something of the wonder and the awe with which a fond mother regards her firstborn."

Watts-Dunton was a man of deep faith, and he believed that God was a "good fellow."

"To word it thus may sound profanely to some ears," commented Watts-Dunton, "but old Khayyám was only trying to express in his pagan way–though I suspect there is as much of FitzGerald as of Omar in the rendering–his belief in the loving Fatherhood of

God which is held by every Christian."

One Aspect of the Many-Sidedness of Theodore Watts-Dunton

Watts-Dunton was a man of great loyalty, and he defended his friends ferociously.

"Of old, certain men and women were supposed to be possessed of the "evil eye." Upon whom they looked with intent–be it man, woman, or beast–hurt was sooner or later sure to fall."

"If there be anything in the superstition, one might almost believe that its opposite was true of Watts-Dunton. He looked upon others merely to befriend, and if he did not put upon them the spell, not of an evil but of a good eye, he exercised a marvellous personal power, not, as is generally the case, upon weaker intellects and less marked personalities than his own, but upon his peers; and even upon those whom in the world's eye would be accounted greater than he."

"Watts is a hero of friendship," Mr. William Michael Rossetti once said of him–and by the passionate personal loyalty of which I have never known the equal. By nature the kindest of men, shrinking from giving pain to any living creature, he could be fierce, even ferocious, to those who assailed his friends."

The Last Days of Theodore Watts-Dunton

Watts-Dunton had outlived nearly all his friends, but he still took great pleasure in his remaining companions. "The pathetic side of the last two or three years of Watts-Dunton's life was that he had outlived nearly every friend of youth and middle age, and, with the one or two old friends of his own generation who survived, he had lost touch."

"It was between Swinburne and Mr. Gosse that the intimacy existed, though by both the inmates he was to the last held in high regard. Mr. Gosse would have the world to believe that he grows old, but no one who knows him either personally or by his writings can detect any sign of advancing years. On the contrary, both in the brilliance of his personality and of his later intellectual achievements, he appears to possess the secret of eternal youth."

"Mr. Thomas Hake was with Watts-Dunton to the end, and indeed it was not a little due to the help of "The Colonel" (the name by which from his boyhood Mr. Hake was known at The Pines on account of his cousinship with and his likeness to Colonel, afterwards General Charles Gordon) that Watts-Dunton accomplished so much literary work in his last decade."

In later life, Watts-Dunton's most treasured friendship was with Sir William Robertson Nicoll.

"Of all the friendships which Watts-Dunton formed late in life none was so prized by him as that with Sir William Robertson Nicoll."

"As we were parting, Watts-Dunton said to me: 'You are coming to lunch on Monday. I wish I could persuade our friend Nicoll here to accompany you, so that Swinburne could share the pleasure of such another meeting as we have had here to-day.'"

"Thereafter, and to his life's end, Watts-Dunton could never speak too gratefully or too appreciatively of Sir William Robertson Nicoll."

In his later years, Watts-Dunton's life was full of happiness, largely due to his marriage. "It was then that the one who was more than friend, the woman he so truly loved, who as truly loved him, became his wife. In his marriage, as in his friendships, Watts-Dunton was singularly fortunate."

"When last I saw them together–married as they had then been for many years–it was evident that Watts-Dunton had lost nothing of the wonder, the awe, perhaps even the perplexity, with which from his boyhood and youth he had regarded that mystery of mysteries–womanhood."

"His love for her was deep, tender, worshipping and abiding, albeit it had something of the fear with which one might regard some exquisite wild bird which, of its own choice, comes to the cage, and, for love's sake, is content to forgo its native woodland, content even to rest with closed wings within the cage, while without comes continually the call to the green field, the great hills and the glad spaces between sea and sky."

"This marriage between a young and beautiful woman–young enough and beautiful enough to have stood for a picture of his adored Sinfi Lovell of *Aylwin*, whom, in her own rich gypsy type of beauty, Mrs. Watts-Dunton strangely resembled–and a poet, novelist, critic and scholar who was no longer young, no longer even middle-aged, was from first to last a happy one."

"The last time I saw Watts-Dunton alive was shortly before his death. I had spent a long afternoon with Mrs. Watts-Dunton and himself, and at night he and I dined alone, as his wife had an engagement. In my honour he produced a bottle of his old "Tennyson" port, lamenting that he could not join me as the doctor had limited him to soda-water or barley-water."

"But, his soulless drink notwithstanding, I have never known him talk more brilliantly. He rambled from one subject to another, not from any lack of power to concentrate or lack of memory, but because his memory was so retentive and so co-ordinating that the mention of a name touched, as it were, an electric button in his memory, which called up other associations."

"Our intercourse that evening was in fact more of a monologue, on his part, than of the usual conversation between two old friends, with interests and intimates in common."

"I am always glad to remember that on this, my last meeting with Watts-Dunton, he was–though evidently weakening and ailing in body–intellectually at his best."

"Come again soon, dear fellow. Come again soon," he said, as he held my hand in a long clasp. And when I had passed out of his sight and he out of mine, his voice followed me pathetically, almost brokenly into the night, "Come again soon, Kernahan. Come again soon, dear boy. Don't let it be long before we meet again."

"It was not long before we met again, but it was, alas, when I followed to his long home one who, great as was his fame in the eyes of the world as poet, critic, novelist and thinker, is, in the hearts of some of us, who grow old, more dearly remembered as the most unselfish, most steadfast, and most loving of friends."

When Stephen Phillips Read

Stephen Phillips was a man of great sensitivity. He would only read poetry in the company of close friends, for the presence of strangers would often make him self-conscious.

"I couldn't help it. That man or that woman's very presence spoilt everything and put me off. I seemed to feel his or her cold and fish-like eyes fastened upon me as I read. I was all the time as aware of that person's boredom as sailors are aware, by the change in the coldness of the atmosphere, of approaching bergs. Worse, I was like a skater, fallen into a hole under the ice; who can find no way out, but is held down and drowned under a roof of solid and unbroken ice."

He possessed a rare and beautiful gift.

"His voice was musical and his elocution that of a consummate artist. But this we had realised before. It was not the charm of his diction that enthralled us, but the melody of his verse–fresh and pure from the heavenly spring."

"His genius was more supremely evident at such times–that is to say, when he was *living* poetry, when he was, as it were, caught up and filled by some Pentecostal spirit of poetry outside himself–than when he was, in travail and labour, if under the pure impulse of inspiration, creating poetry."

"His soul seemed scarcely less far-removed from us, and from our little world, than are the newly dead. For though to no mortal has the soul of a man been visible, to some of us who have listened to Stephen Phillips in those rare moments, it seemed as if *the soul of a man had at least become audible*. Then, in some vague way, one's thoughts wandered back to the time when God walked in the Garden in the cool of the evening, and His Voice was heard by mortals."

"His voice, when he was deeply stirred by poetry, there was something measured, unhasting, majestic, like the vastness of great waters, moving in flood of full tide under the moon."

"Some godlike spirit, outside himself, seemed, in these supreme and consecrated hours, suddenly to possess him, and, when the hour and the consecration were past, as suddenly to leave him."

"While that hour lasted, there was only one word for Stephen Phillips, poet, and that word was Genius."

Edward Whymper as I Knew Him

Edward Whymper was a man of many eccentricities. He enjoyed solitary walks, and found the company of most people to be unbearable. "When in London I was first introduced to him, he and I fell out upon the subject. Hearing that I lived at Southend, he asked me whether I did not agree with him that nowhere else would one meet such objectionable folk as those who journeyed backward and forward to town."

He was a man of routine. Every day, he would make his way to London on the train, where he would eat dry biscuits and drink from a flask before settling down with his work.

"The morning train to town is on the point of starting, the guard has waved his flag, blown his whistle, and is urging late comers to "hurry up." Along the platform, indifferent to the guard's frantic arm-waving, never lengthening his step by so much as one inch, never quickening his pace by as much as by one second, but strolling as leisurely as if the train were not to start for an hour, and looking at each carriage for the face he is seeking, walks a closely-knit, sturdily-built man of middle height."

Whymper was not a man of great friendships. He found the company of others to be irksome, but was often kind to strangers.

"Edward Whymper was a man of few friends, I had almost written of no friends, for though he was upon what, in the case of another man, would be described as terms of friendship with many of the world's most distinguished workers, and though he enjoyed their company and their intercourse as they enjoyed his, I should describe the bond which held him and them together as "liking" and interest in each other and in each other's achievements rather than as friendship in the closer sense of the word."

"That, as I now know, though I was unaware of it at the time, was the surest passport to his favour. Rude even to bearishness as he could on occasion be, Whymper would sometimes go out of his way to show courtesy and even to enter into conversation with an entire stranger. But in all such cases *the advance must come from him.* If it came from the other, he was at once on his dignity, withdrawing as instantly into his shell as an alarmed snail."

Whymper was a man of great knowledge. His interests included geology, mountaineering, and the workings of aneroids.

"Of his mountaineering experiences he said but little, and never once during the thirteen years that I knew him did he of his own accord refer to the historic Matterhorn tragedy. He did, however, tell me of the circumstances under which he became a mountaineer."

"When I was ordered out I wrote to the Primate and asked him to write out a short prayer. I had some thousand copies printed and distributed."

"'One,' repeated Whymper. 'Two,' insisted the other. Then Whymper joined the two halves."

"The question was how to do it and whom to get to do it. To-day they'd do it by photography; but photography wasn't then what it is now, and it was evident that their man would have to be a capable draughtsman, and that he'd have to be a man of nerve, stamina and power of endurance, as he also would have to do some climbing. Well, to cut a long story short, some one who had chanced to see my work in art and to think well of it, suggested me as a likely man. I was glad of a job and jumped at it, but once having started climbing, as I necessarily had to, in six months I had climbed peaks that no one else had ever attempted; and that is the history in brief, if not the whole story, of how I became a climber."

Whymper was a solitary man, but he was also a man of great kindness. He was a generous giver to charities and would often go out of his way to help the poor and needy.

"It was Robert Montgomery, I believe, who wrote a poem in which he pictured the tragic loneliness of "the last man" left alone in the world."

"A man who can so isolate himself is possibly to be envied, even if it never occurred to him that he is also to be pitied. Yet in spite of the fact that he was perfectly satisfied with his lot in life, and in living that life according to the cut-and-dried system by which he ordered it, and in spite, too, of the fact that he would have assured one that he was, and indeed believed himself to be, a happy man, Edward Whymper was, as I have said, not only the loneliest but the most pathetic human creature I have ever known."

"While the professional mendicant was sternly and mercilessly shown the door, the deserving poor he was always, if stealthily and secretly, ready to help."

Whymper was a man of great integrity and honour.

"He was not only as good as his word, but was the soul of integrity and honour. Prepared as he was to fulfil his share of the contract to the letter, he expected and required that others should do the same."

"'I am thirsty and want a drink, please.'" "Are you *bona fide* travellers?" inquired the fellow. "Well," remarked Whymper partly to the fellow and partly to me, "there was a time early in my career when some doubts were cast upon my qualifications as a mountaineer and even, upon my word, in regard to my statement as to what had happened, but, this is the first time I have been challenged in regard to my being a *bona fide* traveller. I'll say nothing about the qualification of my friend here, but considering that since the last time I passed this hostelry I have travelled some seven or eight thousand miles, I think I'm entitled to describe myself as a traveller in a very *bona fide* sense. As a matter of fact, we have come from Southend this morning, which I believe is outside the statutory three miles. Do I look, my good fellow, like a man who'd tell you a lie about a thing like that?"

Whymper was a man of great discipline. He was often seen walking with a small child.

"He had been to town, and, as I was walking towards the station to purchase an evening paper, I saw him stalking in front of me, arrayed in a black greatcoat and top hat and black leather leggings. In one hand he carried his bag, and by the other he clasped the hand of a tiny girl-child, poorly clad and hatless, whom he stooped to comfort as tenderly as could any woman, and in fact took out his own handkerchief to wipe away her tears. The little mite, who hailed from East London, had been sent by some charitable person for a week by the sea to one of the many Holiday Homes for the Poor in Southend."

"Up and down the cliff s of Southend, Whymper marched the lad, impressing upon him the importance of always going at one steady and uniform rate, never, except under exceptional circumstances when haste was absolutely necessary, forcing the pace or indulging in sprinting; teaching him to walk from the hips mechanically and machine wise, so that no strain was put upon the heart and lungs, and instructing him in the control and use of the breath."

"I have been dying to see you again. When *are* you coming along? Edward Whymper. Feb. 24, 1905."

"To me, as to many others of whom I am aware, he did many kindnesses and showed constant friendliness, and if in the opinion of my readers I seem but ill to have requited these kindnesses and that friendliness, by drawing a faithful rather than a flattering picture of the man as I knew him, it is because he was too sincere, too honest, too genuine, too fearless to wish it otherwise."

Oscar Wilde

Oscar Wilde was a man of great charm.

"It is true there was a flabby fleshiness of face and neck, a bulkiness of body, an animality about the large and pursy lips–which did not close naturally, but in a hard, indrawn and archless line–that suggested self-indulgence, but did not to me suggest vice."

He was also a man of great vanity, but his vanity was never malicious.

"A loin-cloth, a fig-leaf would have offended, but it was so artlessly naked that one merely smiled and passed on. Moreover, it was never a jealous or a malicious vanity. It was so occupied in admiring itself in the mirror that the smile on its face was never distorted into a scowl at sight of another's success."

"Wot's the matter with 'im, sir? Why, wanity. 'Ere, get up–Hoscar Wilde!"

Wilde was not a man of great consistency, and he was often given to playing up to his audience.

"It is not for me publicly to point out Gilbert's inferiority. That would be ungenerous. But no one can blame me, if the fact is patent to all."

"The pictures on show in my bachelor rooms, like the furniture, are not of my selection. If you were wounded by what you saw in the Academy, you would die at sight of one work of art on my walls. It is a hideous and vulgar representation of 'Daniel in the Lions' Den,' done in crude chromo, four colours."

"How awful!" he said. "But I can think of something more awful even than that." "What's that?" I asked. "A poor lion in a den of Daniels," was his reply.

Wilde was a man of great artistic ambition. "Shall I tell you what is my greatest ambition–more even than an ambition–the dream of my life? Not to be remembered hereafter as an artist, poet, thinker, or playwright, but as the man who reclothed the sublimest conception which the world has ever known–the Salvation of Humanity, the Sacrifice of Himself upon the Cross by Christ–with new and burning words, with new and illuminating symbols, with new and divine vision, free from the accretions of cant which the centuries have gathered around it."

"Yes," he went on, "I hope before I die to write the Epic of the Cross, the Iliad of Christianity, which shall live for all time."

The setting of Wilde's sun (which had risen on so fair a prospect, and with such promise of splendour) in foul quagmires of sin and shame, was the greatest tragedy I have known.

"God pity him in this hour when human pity there seems none! To think of it! that man, that genius as he is, whom you and I have seen fêted and flattered! whose hand we have grasped in friendship! a felon, and come to infamy unspeakable!"

S.J. Stone, the Hymn-Writer

The Rev. S.J. Stone was a man of great faith. Stone, who wrote the hymns "Weary of earth and laden with my sin" and "The Church's One Foundation," was a man of great nobility and purity.

"To have loved, and to have been loved and trusted by

him, was no less a high privilege than it was a high responsibility, for if any of us, who at some time of our lives, shared Stone's interests and ideals, and were brought under the compelling power and inspiration of his personality, should hereafter come to forget what manner of man he was–should play false with, or altogether fall away, from those ideals, or be content to strive after any less noble standard of conduct and character than he set and attained–then heavy indeed must be our reckoning, in the day when for these, to whom much has been given, much will be required."

He was also a man of great action. He was a lover of sport, and he would often go out of his way to help those in need.

"If he fasted, as was the case during such a season as Holy Week, none knew of it except himself. He held that the season, in which the Church bids us look back in awe and worship upon the agony of our Lord's Passion, is not a time for bodily indulgence by Christ's minister."

"Most of the women in his parish were poor, many pitifully so. Here was a wife toiling all day in a laundry, to keep the home together, while her husband was out of work, or worse still, while her husband was on the drink; and there, a widow, the sole support of several children."

Stone was a man of great loyalty, and he would fight fiercely against those who he saw as enemies of God.

"His own bitterest enemy, Stone

Browsable Glossary

Aylwin *Aylwin*, by Theodore Watts-Dunton, was not only a literary success, it was a critical and commercial phenomenon. The novel appeared in 1898, when Watts-Dunton was a comparatively old man; but, as its reception showed, the world was ready to receive this "delayed" book with open arms. Some of us—though I will not mention names—had read the manuscript many years before, and knew the reasons for its long withholding. Perhaps it is just as well that Mr. Douglas, in his biography of Watts-Dunton, made no mention of this matter, for to have done so would have been to violate a trust.

Baedeker This was the term that the great climber Edward Whymper used to describe himself, as a "Baedeker turned Bradlaugh." It is an amusing if somewhat inaccurate description. Whymper was an accomplished writer. He wrote many travel books, but he was not known as a writer of "guides" for tourists, which was what the term "Baedeker" brought to mind. He wrote, I venture to say, for a more discerning and sophisticated audience.

The Bards Swinburne referred to poets—his contemporaries, and particularly his younger contemporaries—as "bards." I suspect he considered the term as both more courtly and more elevated than the word "poet" itself. He knew, as I also know, that certain of these "bards" were the most sensitive creatures on earth, who, if they had a slight cause for grievance, would never forgive. He must often have smiled, with amused pity, at their self-importance; and must often have wondered—as I have wondered—whether he himself had not given more than one of them an undeserved "bad time."

Beggar my Neighbour This was a name of a village in Yorkshire. I have not the slightest idea whether the name be genuine. I repeat the story merely as it was told me by Swinburne.

The Bend of Passion's Rapids This was George Meredith's description of what constituted, for a man at his best, the supreme moment in life. It is a fine and a memorable phrase.

Berserker-like Laughter This is a term that I, perhaps

out of habit, or perhaps because I am Irish, have often used to describe laughter which is hearty, boisterous, and unrestrained. I am not quite sure whether my usage of it be quite accurate, as "berserker" is a Scandinavian term, and I am not a Scandinavian; but it has the ring of truth.

The Bishop's Mantle S. J. Stone was told by the Bishop of London that, as a hymn-writer, he had inherited the mantle of John Keble. As an Anglican, and as a devout churchman, Stone deeply revered the author of *The Christian Year*. I do not know what the Bishop of London was thinking when he wrote the words. That Stone had inherited the mantle of Keble, I do not believe; and I am sure that Stone himself would never have claimed or thought so for a moment.

Biscuits Whymper, like many other Englishmen, was devoted to biscuits. He ate them habitually on the journey up to town from Southend; he ate them for breakfast, he ate them for supper, and he ate them for lunch. The biscuits, I observed, were always dry, and so, I suppose, were the crumbs.

The Blue This is the term which Englishmen use to describe an honour conferred upon a University oarsman who has had the privilege of rowing against the rival University. In other words, a man who has rowed in the University Boat Race has "got his Blue."

Bloaters Whymper would, I fancy, have been shocked to have heard a fellow creature describe these, his favourite breakfast dish, as "fish." The term "bloater" is perhaps not very elegant, but there is a singular and unforgettable, even poetic suggestiveness about it, for, as every one knows, bloaters are the most salt and succulent of all fish.

The Boarding-house It seems odd that a woman of Madame Sterling's distinction should have been staying at a boarding-house. But, in those days, and even before the war, it was not uncommon for singers and actors to live in boarding-houses, and, in London especially, to make their homes there. The atmosphere of a boarding-house has always seemed to me as incongruous and as unartistic as a church-bell in a music-hall.

Bona Fide Traveller A *bona fide* traveller in the eyes of the law is one who has journeyed three miles from the place where he slept the previous night. To ensure the right to a drink within the prohibited hours, Whymper, as I have said, was prepared to be examined in regard to his bona fides.

The Bow The bow (or bow-wow as it used to be called) was a signal of polite acknowledgment. It was not always the mere bowing of the head, but often involved a bending of the entire body.

The Boxer Rebellion I have heard Whymper speak of

the Boxer Rebellion with unusual bitterness. It was a time when his friend, Admiral Seymour, was in charge of the International Forces at Taku. I imagine Whymper shared the anger of the International Forces at the Boxer's attacks on those, their fellow-creatures, who, in the words of the poet, "lived and moved and had their being" in China, in a land of quaint charm and bewildering contrasts of wealth and poverty.

Brains "Great hearts go generally with great brains," was Swinburne's saying. It is a saying which has always appealed to me, for I have observed that those with the biggest brains are almost invariably the men and women who have the biggest hearts as well.

The British Vagrant This was Whymper's name for the tramp who followed him up Fleet Street after he had thrown him a sixpence. I am not sure whether Whymper was right in thinking that his gift was intended as a "good turn," for the man had been so ragged, so shirtless, and so bootless, that he might very well have been a professional mendicant, who, since he could not be certain of what he would receive, was naturally ready to accept even a sixpence.

The Brute Stevenson held that it was a good thing in the way of character to have "a healthy dash of the brute." I agree. But those who possess this "dash" may be pardoned for sometimes thinking of it, and remembering it, with an uneasy sense of misgiving lest one day it should escape their control.

Bumbledom Bumbledom in its most familiar sense was the name given to the officialdom and the vested interests which, in times past, ruled Poor Law Institutions. It might well be applied, as I have said, to certain Parish Councils and public bodies, and those who are familiar with such bodies will recognise the type to which I refer.

Cambridge Cambridge is one of the two Universities that are supposed to be "rivals." Oxford is the other. A "Blue" from either Oxford or Cambridge is a coveted distinction. It is no less coveted to-day than in times past, though the fashion of wearing caps, or gowns, or "Blues," as of old, has fortunately been discarded.

Cant Cant, as Wilde said, is the great enemy of religion, and of all that is truest, noblest, and most beautiful in human thought and life.

Carniola This is the title given by Watts-Dunton to a novel upon which he was working to the last, but which he never completed. The original name for the book was *Balmoral*.

Casabianca This is the name of the ship which is the subject of the poem of the boy, who, in spite of the fire around him, and of the fact that the vessel was sinking, refused to leave the burning deck, till his father ordered him to do so. It is a noble poem, but a somewhat foolish one, for, if I am not mistaken, it is against the law of the sea, and even against the rules of good seamanship for an officer or a member of the crew to remain on the bridge when the ship is burning.

The Celtic The Celtic, I repeat, is not unknown even in England. It is to be found in Stone's personality no less than in Swinburne's.

The Charterhouse The Charterhouse is a famous London foundation, which includes a church, almshouses, and a school. It was in this ancient and beautiful institution that Stone died, as in fact he had long desired, for he had been at Charterhouse as a boy and had always loved the place. The Charterhouse is to be found in one of Dickens's novels, *The Old Curiosity Shop*, in which it is called "Mr. Sampson's," and the reader will remember the somewhat sinister if not "creepy" character of Mr. Sampson.

Cheyne Walk Cheyne Walk is a street of famous associations in Chelsea, and in those days was especially known as the abode of men and women of letters, and more than one great artist as well. The house at 16 Cheyne Walk, which was then the home of Watts-Dunton and his friend Rossetti, was a place of pilgrimage for many of those who were lovers of literature and art.

Chianti This was a favourite wine of Wilde's. In the

first letter I received from him, he suggested that we should both wear morning dress, and that we should drink "chianti, yellow or red." I have never been able to discover whether there is chianti, yellow or red. I suspect that Wilde was making fun of my ignorance of the wine trade, just as he made fun of my political views.

Chimborazos and Cotopaxis These are names of the mountains which, as Whymper said, he had ascended in the Andes. The sight of them–to those who have never climbed such peaks–is sufficient to make one turn giddy and faint.

The Christy Minstrel Mr. Gerald Christy was, I repeat, a most important, if not indeed, the most important, figure in the lecture field. He was known as a clever and astute business man, who, in his relations with his "minstrels," never failed to get his own way, as well as to get his own way in the matter of the prices he paid them. His "minstrels" were for the most part as ready to accept his terms as a slave would be, but I am happy to remember that Whymper never took advantage of those, his less fortunate brethren, who were under his control.

The Church Militant and Victorious This is a term that is often used in church services and in sermons to describe the Church triumphant, in the sense that she is fighting, and will continue to fight against evil, until her victory is complete. But it seems to me a somewhat inaccurate and even dangerous term, for the victory, if ever it is to be complete, will not be the victory of the Church, but that of God.

A Churchman The term "Churchman," as used by Stone, is not synonymous with "clergyman." There are Churchmen who are not clergymen, as there are clergymen who are not Churchmen. To Stone "Churchman" meant a believer in the doctrines of the Anglican Catholic Church.

Cloughing The term "Cloughing" (it is a somewhat vulgar word) is a good one, and I have often used it, not only in conversation, but in writing, to describe the method by which, by systematic "trailing," snubbing, or contradicting, one succeeds in inducing an egoist, who is talking of nothing but himself, to give his attention to some other subject, and to talk of it.

The Cobwebs Stone called the dry bones of the long-neglected City church "cobwebs," which suggests a picture of neglect, decay, and gloom.

Cold Supper This is an excellent expression, and is the one and only term by which, when one is really hungry, such a supper should be described. It is, too, the best and the truest and the most accurate term.

A Colonial Bishopric Stone, as I have said, declined a Colonial Bishopric. He was too English, too devoted to his own Church, too much in love with his own people. His life-work, the work of which he was intensely proud, was to be done at home, and his one wish was to die in England.

The Communicants Stone used the word "communicants" to describe those members of his congregation who had been confirmed. That the congregation at St. Paul's, Haggerston, included 537 communicants will give some idea of the extent of his influence.

The Consecrated Bread of the Sacrament This was a phrase used by Stone in describing how reverently Swinburne took the flowers offered to him. It shows, I think, that to Stone all such matters were truly symbolic.

The Contemporary Review This was the periodical in which Robert Buchanan's famous article *The Fleshly School of Poetry* was published. The article, written anonymously and even, as it turned out, pseudonymously, was a slashing attack upon Rossetti. It was a controversy which lasted for many years and which—though I am of opinion it was preposterously unjust—caused much grief and trouble.

A Creature of Habit Wilde, as I have said, was something of a "creature of habit." He was fond of good wine, good food, and the best of cigarettes. He was fond, too, of his own well-tried jokes, his own well-tried opinions, and even of his own well-tried phrases.

A Creature of Mood This was a term often used to describe a poet—and not always accurately, for, except for the moods of exaltation and of inspiration, which are not infrequently the outcome of what is called, I think somewhat vaguely, "genius"—a poet's moods, if he be a poet indeed, are, for the most part, and should be, the moods of the moment, fleeting and transitory, just as are the moods of the wind and the seas, which one day are turbulent, and on another placid and still.

The Crevasse A crevasse is a yawning chasm, an ice-filled fissure in a glacier. Whymper, as I have said, had a special gift for descriptive language, and his description of a crevasse as "yawning like a blue hell below" will give the reader some idea of his gifts.

Cromwell Whymper, in replying to Mr. Clodd's comment upon this paper, quoted Cromwell's saying: "Paint me, warts and wrinkles and all." The saying was apt, and Mr. Clodd was right. Whymper would have wished, or at least would have been content, to see himself pictured just as he was, with all his strength and his weakness, his beauty and his ugliness, his nobility and his meanness.

The Cul-de-sac of Despair This was a description, made by me, of Atheism. I am aware that the term is perhaps too strong. It was a term which occurred to me in the moment. I am not sure that it is an accurate description of Atheism. It is true that many, perhaps most, of the men and women who reject the Christian faith are, for the time being, miserable; but misery does not necessarily mean despair. There is, it seems to me, a world of difference between the man or woman, who, rejecting the consolations and assurances of Christianity, chooses to live in the fear and the shadow of annihilation, and the man or woman who has so utterly cast aside all hope and belief in an unseen God and in a future life, that they are able, with smiling fortitude, to meet Death as they meet a friend, and to face annihilation with a quiet mind, as one faces an untroubled sleep.

The "Damned Merit" The courtier of whom Stone was speaking had small idea of the extent to which he was giving utterance to a universal truth. We are all, if I am not mistaken, inclined to feel more strongly against the "merit" which has been earned by conspicuous effort, than for the merit which has been conferred by birth, chance, or accident.

The Dash of the Brute This was, as I have said, Stevenson's term. He was a strong man himself, a man who gloried in his physical strength, a lover of the open air, and of everything natural and virile. It is not the brutish and brutal side of man, the savage and cruel, that he had in mind, but that "dash of the brute" which gives strength and stamina, to those who are called to live adventurous lives, and to battle against adversity.

The Deck-Chair The deck-chair, as is evident from the story of Wilde's encounter with the interviewer, was not only a piece of furniture, but was as much a part of the equipment of the interviewer as his "Baedeker," his notebook, and his pen.

The Degenerate Country This was Wilde's description of England, and of the English people. He found, he said, that England was becoming more and more vulgar. I do not know whether he was right in his view, but he was a clever and witty man, whose every word, even when spoken lightly, was provocative.

The Devil's Doctrine This was my description to Wilde of the doctrine, "The only way to get rid of a temptation is to yield to it." It is a doctrine which has been held for many centuries, even in Christian churches; but it was, as Wilde himself admitted, "damnable."

The "Devil's Weapon" This is Stone's description of satire. It seems to me a somewhat extreme term, for satire is often used to castigate vice, to expose folly, and to pillory sham. Satire is, indeed, one of the weapons which the world uses for purification.

The Devil was Well This is the name of a story which Stevenson was anxious to write. Its scene was to be Italy, in the time of the Renaissance. It is odd that

Stevenson should have been drawn to this particular period, for, with his keen and critical love of the beautiful, it was not a period in history of which he had any high opinion. He described it as "dark, brutal, and dissolute," and, though never a Puritan, he was a man of fine taste and delicate sensibilities. I believe that he planned the story under the influence of some such "evil spirit" as that which, in his other story *Dr. Jekyll and Mr. Hyde*, he pictured as gaining control over the mind of his hero and compelling him, by an unnatural force, to do wrong, and even to commit crime and murder.

The Dickens Friend The "Dickens Friend" was a brother Savage and a lover of all things Dickensian. He knew Dickens's novels by heart, and could repeat at length many of the "sayings" of the great novelist. He had not a high opinion of Wilde, whom he considered "a bit of a poseur," and thought that the latter had been right in refusing to enter the Savage Club.

Discipline Discipline, as Lord Roberts held, is not only important for the soldier but for every citizen. The soldier, he said, should be taught to obey, and to obey instantly, but he should also be taught to act independently, and to act with decision and courage, when the exigencies of the moment demand.

Dirce This is a poem by John Ashworth, of which Mr. Locker-Lampson, the original editor of *Lyra Ele-*

gantiarum, had sent a copy to Tennyson. Tennyson, I am told, was so unfavourably impressed by the poem that he remarked: "It is too classical for English taste."

The Divine Note of the Nightingale This is a phrase often used by Mrs. Moulton, but she was, I believe, the first to apply it in writing to Stone's hymns. It is a perfect description of Stone's music, and especially of that soul-stirring anthem, "The Church's One Foundation."

The Don Quixote of Lost Causes, Lost Chances, and Forlorn Hopes It was a somewhat irreverent description of Stone, but it was a description that had its justification, for he was always ready, and always with unselfish purpose, to fight for a lost cause, to champion a forlorn hope, and to stand by those who had fallen into trouble. He was, in fact, the soul of chivalry.

The Dry Bones Stone spoke of the City church of All Hallows, which had been so long neglected, as "dry bones." His simile was apt, for the building was cold, bare, and gloomy. But Stone, when he had the opportunity of making the place into a spiritual garden, threw himself into his work with such energy that, after a few years of labour, the church was transformed.

The Duchess's Honoured Guest This was Wilde's way of referring to himself, and in so doing he was, as usual, "having a shot." It was his idea that to be the honoured guest at a dinner-party in society is the most important, if not indeed, the only event worth living for. There is, if I am not mistaken, some truth in what he said, for in the eyes of the world the men and women who are invited to these functions are regarded with a certain awe, and even reverence.

The Evil Eye The superstition in regard to the "evil eye" is as old as the human race. It is supposed that those who are born with the evil eye can, by a look, direct misfortune and even death upon others. It is an old-world belief which is still held in some parts of the world, and, I dare say, is still alive and potent in some parts of England.

The Evil Spirit The belief in evil spirits, or in what may be called demoniacal possession, is as old as the human race. It has in recent years been derided and ridiculed, and even, I am sorry to say, by some Churchmen. It was, I believe, the late Professor Robertson Smith who, in writing of the supernatural beliefs of the ancient Hebrews, asserted, in his most learned and scientific way, that the Hebrews were not so foolish as to believe in the existence of evil spirits. I am humbly of opinion that, in his own mind, the Professor was correct; but that the Hebrews, and indeed all other men and women in all ages, have, consciously or unconsciously, lived under the shadow and the fear of these powers, I have no doubt. It seems to me that, since the fall of man, the human soul—I do not mean the body—has been, if I may so phrase it, *liable to invasion by these evil spirits.* Those who have never heard, or have never accepted this view, will, I fancy, find themselves in a somewhat uncomfortable position in regard to, let us say, the treatment of insanity by the medical profession, for the medical experts will, I am sure, agree with me that, not infrequently, a man or woman who is insane is either the subject of, or is possessed by, evil spirits.

The Éclat This is a French word which means "splendour." Whymper used it in speaking of the importance which climbers attached to the illustrations in their books.

Eig This is the name of one of the islands in the Hebrides.

The English Mother This was Stone's description of Queen Victoria, whom he worshipped as his Sovereign, and whom he also revered as his Mother.

The English Sporting Spirit Whymper, if I am not mistaken, was not, in the strict sense of the word, a sportsman. But he was intensely patriotic, and he was prepared, if need be, to go to any lengths to defend his country. "To carry on a war and to fight a war are two very different things," he once said to me. "One is the work of the politician; the other is the work of the soldier, and the true soldier has something of the sportsman in him."

The English Tongue Stone's hymns are sung wherever the English language is spoken. That is a great and a memorable fact. But I sometimes wonder whether Stone would have been quite so proud of his hymns had he been aware that, though to us, the English language is as sacred as a Bible, it is not so held by other peoples. My friend, the late Colonel F. G. Bettany, once wrote a very charming little book concerning the origin and growth of the English tongue; and if I remember rightly he made this observation: "The English language has a noble history, and is, in itself, a beautiful and harmonious instrument of speech; but when we boast of it as the language of the world, we are simply taking an unwarrantable and even offensive assumption to ourselves."

Enoch Arden This is the hero of Tennyson's *Enoch Arden*. Stone was quoting Tennyson's poem, in which, he said, was described the "faith" which kept Enoch Arden, in spite of the terrible news that had reached him of the death of his wife, from being "all unhappy."

An Erratum Slip This is a printed slip inserted in a book to correct an error.

An Essay in Miniature This is how Watts-Dunton described his letters. His letters, though sometimes lengthy, were, he said, "carelessly and free from the irking consciousness that he was writing for publication." And so, of course, they were. And they are the more beautiful, the more illuminating, and the more valuable for being so.

The Eternal and Omnipotent God This was the phrase used by that other Voice which, in my ear, seemed to refute the tempter's words when I stooped over Stone's dead body.

The Événement This is a French term, meaning "event."

The Evil Influences Wilde was, as I have said, a man whose vanity and desire to be distinguished led him to do many things which he knew to be wrong. The influences by which he was thus misled came, some of them, from those who were his friends, or at least, in the common acceptance of the word, his associates.

The Exasperating Thing about Such Letters This was Swinburne's expression in speaking of the letters received by those who have a reputation in literature. He knew well, as every one knows who has ever had any success as a writer, that these letters are often very hard to deal with. There is something, I admit, of the "pest" about them.

The Expulsion Wilde, in speaking of the "Silence Club" of which I am a member, said that any author who so much as mentioned his own book was unconditionally expelled. Wilde was not above a little jest, but in this case, he was expressing a truth, for, in those days, there was a general feeling among writers that it is bad form to advertise one's work. I remember, in the "golden age" of the *Saturday Review*, that, though an editor of that periodical may have made a good deal of money by reviewing his own novels in its pages, he was censured, even pilloried, for doing so.

The Fancy Wilde's "fancy" was an aphorism–"A gentleman never goes east of Temple Bar." Aphorisms are, I suppose, a good thing in their way. But, to me, they are not in themselves a very high form of literary expression. They are, I admit, sometimes startling, as well as suggestive. But, when carefully examined, they are often no more than the expression of a truth, or the reflection of an existing social condition, or of a mood of the moment, put into one or two neat and pregnant words.

The Fatherhood of God The Fatherhood of God, as Stone would have said, is a "fundamental truth" which no one who believes in Christianity can doubt.

The "Fogey-brother" This was Watts-Dunton's term for F. W. Robinson.

The Foolish Girls and Women This was Stone's way of describing those who sought his help in regard to love-affairs. They were, he held, foolish, since their troubles were, he believed, mainly of their own making, and their troubles did not concern him.

The "Foolish Bogey Story" This was my description of the story that Robert Buchanan's article *The Fleshly School of Poetry* had caused Rossetti to take to drugs, and had even caused his death. The "story" is, as I have said, a "foolish bogey story," and to my thinking should be laid to rest forever.

The "Four Colours" Wilde spoke of "Daniel in the Lions' Den," done in crude chromo, four colours, as "hideous and vulgar." I do not know whether he was right. I do not know whether the picture in question existed or was simply an invention of Wilde's.

The "Four and a Half Millions" This is the number that Mr. Winston Churchill, then First Lord of the Admiralty, gave in a memorable speech, as the number of soldiers then available to Germany. He spoke at the same time of the huge sums that were being spent upon the German army and upon the German navy, and said that "if Germany wished to force a war upon England, the only thing which would deter her would be our own preparedness." The speech caused, and has since caused, much controversy.

The "Four-page Essay" This was Watts-Dunton's method of reviewing books in the *Athenæum*, a journal of high intellectual standing.

The "Free Trade Hall" This was the Hall at Manchester, in which, Lord Roberts said, he had spoken plainly about the necessity for National Service.

"The Friar" This was Watts-Dunton's description of the cartoonist Sir F. C. Gould.

A "Friend" Wilde in his letter to me, about my fairy story, referred to himself as my "friend." This, though a common expression, had a significance which to me was not a little impressive, for, in his company, I had often heard him speak disparagingly of the word, and in fact, say that "there are few things more to be feared than a man or a woman who claims to be your friend."

The "Ghastly" Time This was Stone's description of the fortnight he spent at Southend after leaving Haggerston. To him, I may say, there were few more "ghastly" things than the thought of leaving the old parish and the people whom he loved there. He was, I may add, a lover of the sea, and Southend was a sea-side resort. But, I am inclined to think that "ghastly" was a term that occurred to him, partly from physical illness and partly from spiritual depression.

The "Give-and-take" This was a term often used by Watts-Dunton in describing a conversation. The "give-and-take" is, to me, the most important and the most characteristic thing about any conversation, and, when the give-and-take is at its best, it is a thing of beauty. I am not quite sure, however, that Mr. Douglas is right in saying that "for all their smartness, crispness, and epigram, in the work of certain modern novelists, reading whom, one is inclined to wonder whether two ordinary mortals ever did, in real life, rattle off, impromptu, quite so many brilliant repartees, and clever epigrams, in so short a time."

The "Golden Song" This was the title given to my sister's weekly contribution to a well-known periodical. The title itself is somewhat sentimental, but that is a characteristic of religious writing.

The "Good Fellow" "Good fellowship" was to Watts-Dunton the first essential in life. It was, indeed, the very foundation upon which he based his religion. The only people he could not stand—perhaps only because he had no use for them—were those whom he described as "intellectually-little writing fellows who do not matter, and who do not count."

The "Good-fellowship of God" This was an article which Watts-Dunton wanted to write, but never did. It was to be based on Omar Khayyám's lines:

"And daub His Visage with the Smoke of Hell; They talk of some strict testing of us–Pish! He's a Good Fellow and 'twill all be well.

The term "good-fellowship," as applied to God, is of

course, a paradox. But it is a paradox which has its justification, since God, as well as being mighty, is also merciful, and, as I believe Watts-Dunton thought, is a "Good Fellow," if only in the sense that He "takes pleasure in the prosperity of his servants."

The "Goose" Stone compared his friends to swans, and I have already said that he had a habit of idealising them. A "swan" is not, as I have said, any more beautiful in its waddle on land than is a "goose."

The "Graphic" This was an illustrated weekly which included, in a certain number, a "supplement," *Poets of the Day*. The supplement contained portraits, of which Swinburne made entertaining comments.

The Great Man This was the interviewer's description of Wilde. It was, as is customary in the "lionising" fraternity, extravagant; but, nevertheless, it was not altogether untrue.

The Great War This, as has already been said, has changed the whole of life. The war, as I write, is over; but the world, in spite of the fact that the men and women of whom I have written have themselves passed out of it, is still under the spell of its tremendous tragedy.

The Greatness "The greatness was in nearly every case, not inherited but achieved." This was a sentence from an article, which was read aloud to the Prime Minister in the presence of Lord Roberts. It is a fine sentence, in which we have a description of that greatness which has been the heritage of the British people, and that is, in my humble opinion, still its heritage.

The "Greek God" This was Mr. Bleackley's description of Stephen Phillips as an actor. The description was, I admit, not without its exaggeration, but there was no doubt that Phillips had the beauty of a Greek god. His features were, as Mr. Bleackley said, "the features of a Greek god," and that his head was finely formed, I well remember, for I have seen it many times in my lifetime. To-day, a man of beauty in the eyes of others is often thought to be effeminate. In those days–perhaps because the old ideals were still operative, and because, as it seemed to us, a man of beauty was also a man of strength–Phillips's beauty was taken as one of his attributes, as one of the many good things that went to make up a man worthy of the name.

Grub Street "Grub Street" is a slang term which was once used to denote the abode of literary men, especially of those of small merit and in pecuniary straits. To-day, it is used by those who follow the craft of Letters as a term of endearment, and, in the sense that we all, writers as we are, more or less live by picking each other's brains, there is a certain grim truth in it.

The Gutter This was the "editor's" term, in the story told by Watts-Dunton, for the place where the author was supposed to be "selling his papers." It is, as I have said, a term that has passed into slang, and I do not know what it meant to the editor in question when he used it.

The Haggerston This was the parish in London in which Stone had lived and worked for a long time, and where he had many friends. He was, I may say, intensely fond of this, his first parish. He referred to it

Timeline

1875: Robert Louis Stevenson writes to Sir Sidney Colvin about his next story, *When the Devil was Well*.

1885: The first number of *Home Chimes* appears, featuring poems by both Swinburne and Watts-Dunton.

1890: S. J. Stone resigns from his parish in Haggerston after a breakdown and is appointed rector of All Hallows, London Wall.

1891: Stone writes to Kernahan about his depression after leaving Haggerston.

1891: Watts-Dunton writes to Kernahan about his time with Tennyson at Aldworth, Haslemere.

1892: Kernahan meets Swinburne personally for the first time.

1892: Stone writes to Kernahan about his religious novel.

1892: Wilde writes to Kernahan about his upcoming play *Lady Windermere's Fan*.

1896: Francis Hinde Groome writes to Kernahan about the possibility of Watts-Dunton writing a *Life of Rossetti*.

1897: Whymper writes to Kernahan about his friendship with Tennyson.

1897: Stone writes to Kernahan about the *Lays of Iona*.

1898: *Aylwin* is published, when Watts-Dunton is sixty-six years old.

1899: Stone writes to Kernahan about his friend who has converted to Catholicism.

1899: Stone suffers a breakdown.

1900: Wilde dies in November.

1905: Whymper writes to Kernahan's stepson.

1909: Swinburne dies in April.

1910: Kernahan publishes an article on National Defence in the *London Quarterly Review*.

1910: Lord Roberts writes to Kernahan about the article he has written.

1910: Whymper and Thomas Hardy meet at Mr. Clodd's house.

1913: Lord Roberts writes a lengthy letter to Kernahan to be read at a Brotherhood Meeting in Hastings.

1913: Watts-Dunton celebrates his eighty-first birthday.

1913: Watts-Dunton writes to Kernahan about a watercolor painting of the dining-room at 16 Cheyne Walk, with Rossetti reading out to him the proofs of *Ballads and Sonnets*.

1914: Lord Roberts and Kernahan discuss the prayer mistakenly attributed to the former.

1914: Lord Roberts introduces a deputation advocating National Service to the Prime Minister.

1914: The war breaks out.

1914: Lord Roberts dies on service.

1915: Horace Bleackley writes "An Impression of Stephen Phillips" for the *Outlook*.

1917: *In Good Company* is published.

Milton Keynes UK
Ingram Content Group UK Ltd.
UKHW021124231024
449869UK00016B/440